Roll of Thunder Hear My Cry

L-I-T Guide
Literature In Teaching

By Mildred Taylor

A Study Guide for Grades 4 to 8
Prepared by Charlotte S. Jaffe and Barbara T. Doherty
Illustrated by Karen Sigler

The purchase of this book entitles the individual teacher to reproduce copies of the student pages for use in his or her classroom exclusively. The reproduction of any part of the work for an entire school or school system or for commercial use is prohibited.

ISBN 1-56644-010-6

Revised Edition © 1997 Educational Impressions, Inc., Hawthorne, NJ

EDUCATIONAL IMPRESSIONS, INC.
Hawthorne, NJ 07507

Roll of Thunder, Hear My Cry
Written by Mildred Taylor

STORY SUMMARY

Cassie Logan lived with her three brothers, her parents, and her grandmother in rural Mississippi during the Great Depression of the 1930's. The economy throughout the United States was in terrible shape, and the rural South was hit hardest of all.

Although often the victims of the bigotry and racism that was prevalent at the time, the Logans were determined to maintain their dignity. The family struggled to make ends meet. Unlike most of their neighbors who were sharecroppers, the Logans owned their own land and they wanted desperately to keep it. The land had originally belonged to a white family whose descendants were trying to get it back.

Cassie was a proud, independent, intelligent girl. She was a good student at the all-black, segregated school where her mother taught. Although she wanted very much to please her parents and her grandmother, Cassie also enjoyed the "scrapes" she got into with her brothers.

Life for Cassie and her family was not easy. However, they did their best to lend support to one another and to their neighbors and to deal with the inequities of the world.

Meet the Author
Mildred Taylor

Mildred Taylor was born in Jackson, Mississippi, but spent her childhood and teen years in Toledo, Ohio. Her writings were influenced by family stories that she had heard as a child. "By the fireside in our Ohio home, and in Mississippi where I was born, from as far back as I can remember, my father taught me a different history from the one I learned in school," she once stated.

After graduating from the university of Toledo, Mildred studied and traveled throughout Africa. She spent two years in Ethiopia on assignment with the Peace Corps. Mildred also found time to work with the Black Student Alliance at the University of Colorado, where she pursued graduate studies. "[During this period] I would find myself turning again to the stories I had heard in my childhood. I was deeply drawn to the roots of the inner world which I knew so well," she explained.

Song of the Trees, her first book about the Logan family, was written in 1975. It won the Council of Interracial Books Award. It also was named Outstanding Book of the Year by *The New York Times. Roll of Thunder, Hear My Cry* was written in 1976 and became a Newbery Medal Winner. "In my novels," she wrote, "I wanted to show the black person as heroic. It is my hope that to the children who read my books, the Logans will provide those black heroes missing from the schoolbooks of my childhood."

Tenant Farming and Sharecropping

When the Civil War ended, many planters did not have the money to hire farm laborers; therefore, they began to sell portions of their land. In time, a very small number of freed slaves were able to acquire small farms. A few others—like many poor whites—entered into a relationship known as tenant farming. In a tenant relationship, the planter rented portions of his land to a number of tenants, who paid their rent in the form of a share of their crop—usually one fourth to one third. The tenants provided their own seed, tools and other supplies. Some tenant farmers eventually managed to save enough money to buy their own plot of land.

Related to tenant farming was sharecropping. Most sharecroppers were blacks. Sharecroppers provided only the labor; they were given a cabin, seed, tools and a mule and were expected to work the land for the planter. In return, the sharecroppers were given a percentage of the crop—usually a third to a half. Because the sharecroppers weren't paid until harvest time, they were forced to buy their food and other provisions on credit. Most of their share of the crop went to pay back the loans and the interest that accumulated. In many cases the same person who owned the farm also owned the store at which the sharecroppers were expected to shop. The landowner/shopkeeper became an important figure in the economy of the South.

Mississippi

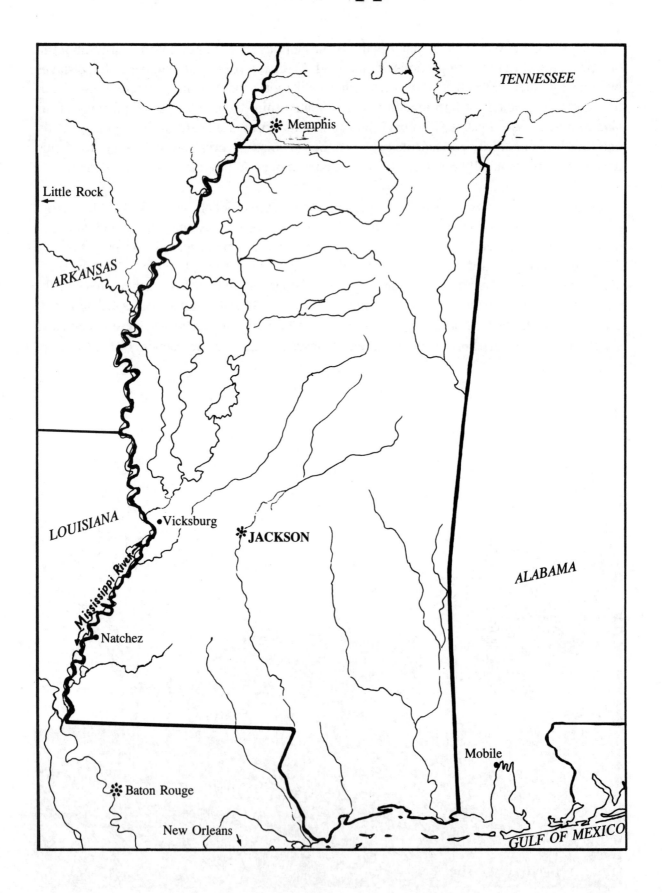

Vocabulary
Chapters One and Two

Match the vocabulary words on the left to the definitions on the right. Place the correct letter on each line.

____ 1. amiably   A. extremely thin, especially from starvation

____ 2. barren   B. delicate; weak; easily broken

____ 3. briar   C. arrogantly

____ 4. chiffonier   D. damage; spoil the quality of

____ 5. emaciated   E. sullenly; gloomily

____ 6. formidable   F. pleasingly; agreeably

____ 7. frail   G. not discouraged

____ 8. ginned   H. dissenter; independent-minded person

____ 9. gleaned   I. briskly; confidently

____ 10. imperiously   J. seriously; thoughtfully

____ 11. jauntily   K. plant with a thorny, woody stem

____ 12. loitering   L. lean and muscular; strong and vigorous

____ 13. mar   M. not productive

____ 14. maverick   N. removed the seeds from cotton

____ 15. morosely   O. lingering idly; wasting time

____ 16. pensively   P. high, narrow chest of drawers

____ 17. raucous   Q. on guard; cautious

____ 18. sinewy   R. gathered little by little

____ 19. undaunted   S. harsh; rough-sounding

____ 20. wary   T. hard to overcome; arousing dread or fear

© Educational Impressions, Inc.

Roll of Thunder, Hear My Cry

Comprehension and Discussion Questions
Chapter One

Answer the following questions in complete sentence form. Give examples from the story to support your response.

1. Why did Papa spend so much time away from the family?

_____
_____
_____
_____

2. Why were Cassie and her brothers first starting school in October?

_____
_____
_____
_____

3. Why did Cassie and her brothers attend a different school from Jeremy and his sister? Contrast the two schools.

_____
_____
_____
_____

4. Explain how Mama reacted to Cassie's and Little Man's refusal to accept the books. Judge this reaction.

_____
_____
_____
_____

8 *Roll of Thunder, Hear My Cry* © Educational Impressions, Inc.

Comprehension and Discussion Questions
Chapter Two

Answer the following questions in complete sentence form. Give examples from the story to support your response.

1. Why, do you think, did Papa bring Mr. Morrison to the Logan farm?

_____
_____
_____
_____

2. Why could Papa stay home only one night?

_____
_____
_____
_____

3. How did John Henry Berry die?

_____
_____
_____
_____

4. Why didn't Papa want the children to go to Mr. Wallace's store? The children thought Papa's statement was "disconnected with the conversation." Do you agree?

_____
_____
_____
_____

Vocabulary
Chapters Three and Four

Find the following words in Chapters Three and Four. Use your dictionary to define them based upon their use in the story.

1. aloof: _____
2. caravan: _____
3. careened: _____
4. coddling: _____
5. donned: _____
6. feigned: _____
7. haggard: _____
8. haughtily: _____
9. moronic: _____
10. plaguing: _____
11. riveted: _____
12. veered: _____
13. ventured: _____
14. vex: _____
15. wafted: _____

Word Links

Create word links using as many of the vocabulary words in the first part of this activity as possible. Try to include several vocabulary words for each word link.

EXAMPLE:

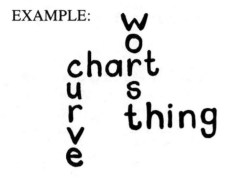

Comprehension and Discussion Questions
Chapter Three

Answer the following questions in complete sentence form. Give examples from the story to support your response.

1. Little Man seemed to get more upset than the other children when they were muddied by the schoolbus driver. Why?

_____
_____
_____
_____

2. Why, do you suppose, didn't Jeremy Simms ever ride the schoolbus with the other white children?

_____
_____
_____
_____

3. Describe Stacey's secret plan for revenge against the bus driver and the children on the bus. What important fact did the children fail to consider that made them feel a little guilty afterward?

_____
_____
_____
_____

4. Why did Mr. Avery's visit frighten Cassie and her brothers?

_____
_____
_____
_____

Comprehension and Discussion Questions
Chapter Four

Answer the following questions in complete sentence form. Give examples from the story to support your response.

1. Why did Stacey sigh with relief when T.J. told them why the "night riders" had tarred and feathered Mr. Tatum?

_____
_____
_____
_____

2. Why was Stacey punished in class? Do you think he should have taken the punishment or do you think he should have explained what really happened?

_____
_____
_____
_____

3. Why did Mr. Morrison announce that he would not tell their mother that the Logan children had been to the Wallaces' store?

_____
_____
_____
_____

4. What was Mrs. Logan's purpose for taking the children to visit the Berrys?

_____
_____
_____
_____

Vocabulary
Chapters Five and Six

Find the following words in Chapters Five and Six. Use your dictionary to define them based upon their use in the story.

1. ambled: _____
2. balked: _____
3. bland: _____
4. faltered: _____
5. languidly: _____
6. malevolently: _____
7. nattily: _____
8. obnoxious: _____
9. reverently: _____
10. reprimand: _____
11. reluctantly: _____
12. retaliated: _____
13. subdued: _____
14. sullenly: _____
15. sulked: _____

Choose eight of the above words and write an original sentence for each.

_____
_____
_____
_____
_____
_____
_____
_____

Comprehension and Discussion Questions
Chapter Five

Answer the following questions in complete sentence form. Give examples from the story to support your response.

1. Why did Cassie like Mr. Jamison?

2. Why was Cassie upset with Mr. Barnett? Do you think Cassie's behavior was justified?

3. Why wasn't Stacey concerned about leaving T.J. alone in Barnett's Mercantile?

4. Why, do you think, did Big Ma tell Cassie to apologize to Lillian Jean? How would you have felt if you were Cassie?

Comprehension and Discussion Questions
Chapter Six

Answer the following questions in complete sentence form. Give examples from the story to support your response.

1. Cassie felt that Big Ma should have stood up for her against Mr. Simms. Do you agree? Explain.

_____
_____
_____
_____

2. Describe Hammer's reaction to Mama's plea that he not make "unnecessary trouble."

_____
_____
_____
_____

3. According to Mama, why did people like Mr. Simms cling to the belief that white people were better than black people?

_____
_____
_____
_____

4. What did Mama mean when she said, "One day we'll pay for it. Believe me."

_____
_____
_____
_____

Vocabulary
Chapters Seven and Eight

Use the words in the box to complete the sentences below. You may need to use your dictionary.

> adorned acknowledged astonishment bewildered briskly condoned
> confided denotes distastefully encounter flaunting glittered inaudible
> interjected obvious prophesied resentful sentinels wary wry

1. The baby was _____ by the confusing noises of the crowd.
2. The boys met at the mall. It was an unexpected _____.
3. It was _____ that the dry plants needed watering.
4. Her _____ sense of humor amused the visitors.
5. The children glanced _____ at T.J. for his mean remarks.
6. He carefully _____ the tree with colorful ornaments.
7. The _____ guarded the fortress.
8. Her soft voice was _____ in the large and crowded room.
9. The new student was _____ her expensive clothes to impress the class.
10. A look of _____ crossed his face when he heard the surprising news.
11. The cold wind moved _____ through the leafless trees.
12. Cassie was _____ because Mama was told to leave her job.
13. A grade of A _____ excellent work.
14. The speaker _____ humor into his speech.
15. The coach _____ the pitcher's efforts by giving him the MVP award.

Some of the words in the vocabulary box were not used. Write an original sentence for each of those words.

_____
_____
_____
_____

© Educational Impressions, Inc.   Roll of Thunder, Hear My Cry

Comprehension and Discussion Questions
Chapter Seven

Answer the following questions in complete sentence form. Give examples from the story to support your response.

1. Compare and contrast the reactions of Uncle Hammer and Mama when they learned that Stacey had given away his coat.

_____
_____
_____
_____

2. What kind of mood did the author create when she described Christmas at the Logan home? Name specific factors that helped create this mood.

_____
_____
_____
_____

3. Why did Papa think it was important for the children to listen to Mr. Morrison's tales about slavery?

_____
_____
_____
_____

4. Why did Harlan Granger visit the Logans?

_____
_____
_____
_____

Comprehension and Discussion Questions
Chapter Eight

Answer the following questions in complete sentence form. Give examples from the story to support your response.

1. What advice did Papa offer to Cassie about her relationship with Lillian Simms?

___

2. How did Cassie get even with Lillian? Did she heed her father's advice? Explain.

___

3. How did Mr. Granger get his revenge on Mama?

___

4. According to Little Willie, who was to blame for Mama's being fired? How did Stacey get revenge?

___

© Educational Impressions, Inc.

Roll of Thunder, Hear My Cry 19

Vocabulary
Chapters Nine and Ten

Find the following words in Chapters Nine and Ten. Use your dictionary to define them based upon their use in the story.

1. adamantly
2. amenities
3. condescending
4. despairingly
5. despondently
6. exasperation
7. furrowed
8. indefinitely
9. ledger
10. lethargically
11. mortgage
12. overshadow
13. persistent
14. premature
15. resigned
16. scheme
17. self-consciously
18. summon
19. unison
20. urgency

Send a Letter

Pretend that you are Papa and write a letter to your brother Hammer. Tell him of the need to save the Logan land. Use at least eight vocabulary words from the first part of this activity in your letter.

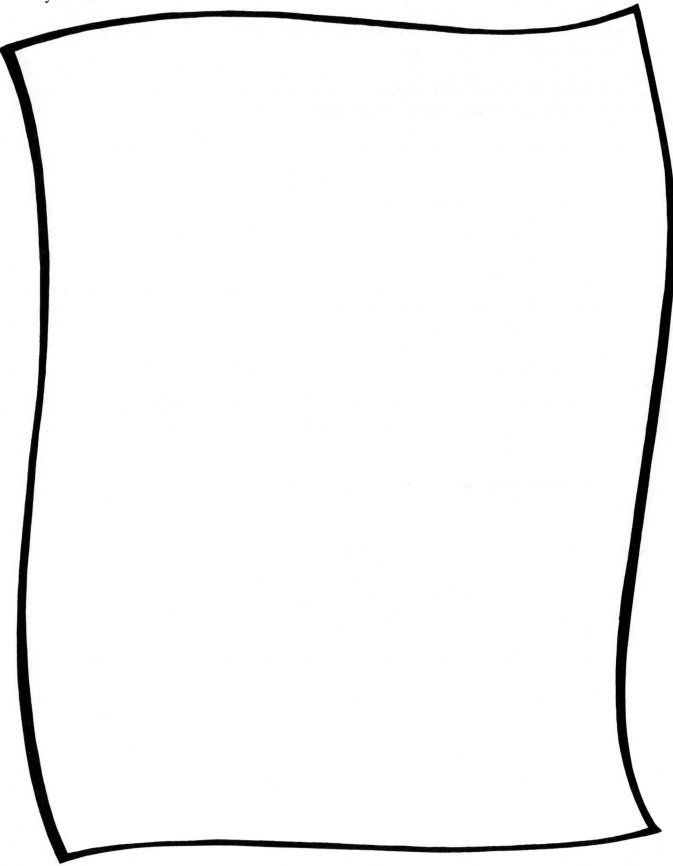

Comprehension and Discussion Questions
Chapter Nine

Answer the following questions in complete sentence form. Give examples from the story to support your response.

1. Why did Mr. Jamison want to speak to David Logan? Would you consider Mr. Jamison a friend if you were a member of the Logan family? Explain.

_____
_____
_____
_____

2. Why did Mr. Avery and Mr. Lanier change their minds about making the Vicksburg trip? Do you think they made the right decision? Explain.

_____
_____
_____
_____

3. Why, do you think, did Papa want Stacey to go with him to Vicksburg?

_____
_____
_____
_____

4. Stacey blamed himself for Papa's broken leg. Do you agree with his reasoning?

_____
_____
_____
_____

Comprehension and Discussion Questions
Chapter Ten

Answer the following questions in complete sentence form. Give examples from the story to support your response.

1. Why did Mama and Papa agree not to tell Hammer about their financial woes? What caused Papa to change his mind?

_____
_____
_____
_____

2. Why was Mr. Morrison confident that Mr. Wallace would not hurt him or the children?

_____
_____
_____
_____

3. Were you surprised that Uncle Hammer sold his car? Explain.

_____
_____
_____
_____

4. Why, do you think, did T.J. bring R.W. and Melvin to the revival?

_____
_____
_____
_____

Comprehension and Discussion Questions
Chapter Eleven

Answer the following questions in complete sentence form. Give examples from the story to support your response.

1. Why did the Logan children decide to take home the injured T.J.?

_____
_____
_____
_____

2. Why, do you think, didn't they tell their family about taking T.J. home? What would you have done in their situation? Explain.

_____
_____
_____
_____

3. How did Mr. Jamison and the sheriff prevent the crowd from hanging T.J.?

_____
_____
_____
_____

4. Why was it imperative that Papa and Mr. Morrison be told about what had happened at the Avery home?

_____
_____
_____
_____

Vocabulary
Chapters Eleven and Twelve

Part One: Choose the word in each set that is **most like** the first word in meaning.

1. **recitation:** recipe   oration   listing
2. **trudge:** plod   scamper   run
3. **interminable:** brief   curt   prolonged
4. **billowed:** surged   shrank   yelled
5. **remnants:** leftovers   additions   supplements
6. **savagely:** violently   calm   knowingly
7. **menacingly:** kindly   bravely   threateningly
8. **vulnerability:** safety   defenselessness   security

Part Two: Choose the word in each set that is **most unlike** the first word in meaning.

1. **crescendo:** increase   decrease   melody
2. **emerge:** evacuate   exit   enter
3. **affirmation:** denial   confirmation   declaration
4. **gruffly:** sternly   mildly   harshly
5. **despicable:** likable   contemptible   hateful
6. **solemnly:** seriously   gravely   lightheartedly
7. **oblivious:** aware   unmindful   forgetful
8. **suspiciously:** distrustfully   trustingly   skeptically

© Educational Impressions, Inc.

Roll of Thunder, Hear My Cry

Headliners

Use the vocabulary words from the first part of this activity to create three headlines. Use at least one vocabulary word (or a form of the word) per headline. Try to use more!

Example: **Grim Facts Emerge from Investigation of Mercantile Fraud**

Comprehension and Discussion Questions
Chapter Twelve

Answer the following questions in complete sentence form. Give examples from the story to support your response.

1. Why were Papa and Mama angry when the children first returned to the house? Why did they change their feelings after they had heard the children's story?

2. Why was Mr. Jamison afraid for Papa to go into town after the fire? Do you think the fire was a good idea? Give reasons for your opinion.

3. What do you think T.J.'s punishment was? Do you think his punishment fit his crime? Explain.

4. Based upon the conclusion of the story, do you think that the Logans' situation will improve or worsen? Explain.

Spotlight Literary Skill
Characterization

Mildred Taylor, the author of *Roll of Thunder, Hear My Cry,* stated that she created the Logan family in order to provide the African-American heroes that were missing from the schoolbooks that she had read as a child. How has she made the characters seem heroic? Next to each character's name, write at least one example of his or her courageous behavior.

HEROES AND HEROINES

Cassie

Stacey

Papa

Mama

Big Mama

Little Man

Hammer

Spotlight Literary Skill
Compare and Contrast

In your readings, you will often notice differences and similarities among characters, settings and events. When you are asked to *compare things, you must analyze the ways that those things appear to be the same. In other words, you tell how one thing is like another similar thing. When you are asked to **contrast** things, you must carefully consider the ways the things appear to be different. In other words, you tell about the differences between the two similar things.

Use the information you learned from reading *Roll of Thunder, Hear My Cry* to compare and contrast the following characters and places.

	COMPARE	**CONTRAST**
Papa and Hammer		
Stacey and T.J.		
Great Faith Elementary School and Jefferson Davis Country School		
Mr. Granger and Mr. Jamison		
Mama and Big Ma		

*Note: *Compare* is sometimes used to include differences as well as similarities.

Spotlight Literary Skill
Point of View

Point of view is the voice that is used to tell the story plot. Some stories have a first person narrator. **A first person narrator** is the character who tells the story. That character refers to himself or herself as I and takes part in the story. In this story, Cassie is the first person narrator.

Sometimes a story event can change when told from different points of view. With members of your cooperative learning group, describe the terrifying events of Chapter Eleven from the point of view of each of the characters listed below.

TERROR AT THE AVERY HOUSE!

Stacey's Point of View:

Mr. Jamison's Point of View:

Kaleb Wallace's Point of View:

Mr. Avery's Point of View:

Melvin Simms's Point of View:

T.J.'s Point of View:

Cooperative Learning Activity
Creating Chapter Titles

The twelve chapters of *Roll of Thunder, Hear My Cry* are untitled. Discuss the highlights of each chapter with the members of your Cooperative Learning Group and brainstorm ideas for original titles. Write the final choice for each chapter in the left column. Give your reasons for each choice in the column on the right. Compare your results with those of the other groups in the class.

	TITLES	REASONS FOR CHOICE
Chapter One		
Chapter Two		
Chapter Three		
Chapter Four		
Chapter Five		
Chapter Six		
Chapter Seven		
Chapter Eight		
Chapter Nine		
Chapter Ten		
Chapter Eleven		
Chapter Twelve		

Crossword Puzzle
Roll of Thunder, Hear My Cry

See how much you remember about *Roll of Thunder, Hear My Cry*. Have fun!

Across
3. State in which story takes place.
8. What the Logan children got for Christmas.
9. Last name of the man who came to live with the Logans.
10. Stacey gave his new one to T.J.
12. Cassie's uncle.
15. A tenant farmer who gives a share of his crop to the landlord.
16. Cassie was forced to apologize to her. (First Name).
18. R.W. and Melvin told one.
19. Name of the school for whites.
21. The ____ driver muddied the children.
23. Crop grown by the Logans.
24. Papa worked on one.
26. Mr. Tatum was ____ and feathered.
27. What Cassie's youngest brother was called.
29. Middle name of 16 across.
30. Relationship of Papa to Big Ma.

Down
1. Cassie's grandmother.
2. Where Papa and Stacey were coming from when Papa was shot.
3. Author of *Roll of Thunder, Hear My Cry*.
4. Last name of white boy who enjoyed the company of the Logan children.
5. Great Faith was the ____ for black children.
6. Christopher-____ was one of Cassie's brothers.
7. Part of the Logans' fields were destroyed by it.
10. The novel is told from her point of view.
11. He was set afire by the Wallaces.
12. He fired Mama.
13. She was fired for teaching about slavery.
14. What the schools in Mississippi were at the time of this story.
17. There was a lot of this in the Logan household.
20. He backed the credit of the black families so they could shop in Vicksburg.
22. Cassie's oldest brother.
23. Uncle Hammer sold his when the bank called up the note on the Logan farm.
25. Last name of 10 down.
28. Logan's neighbor; he was involved in the robbery of Barnett's Mercantile.

© Educational Impressions, Inc.

More Post-Reading Activities

1. Research and report on the Civil Rights Movement of the 1960's and the provisions of the Civil Rights Act of 1964. Describe how life in the South changed for black Americans as a result.

2. Discuss the terms *prejudice* and *discrimination* with your classmates and teacher. Role-play situations in which these terms may apply. Have classmates relate negative experiences during which they either found themselves to be prejudiced, were victims of prejudice or discrimination, or witnessed an incident of prejudice or discrimination.

3. Read other novels that deal with the same theme. A few suggestions are the following:
   Sounder, by William Armstrong
   The Cay, by Theodore Taylor
   Let the Circle Be Unbroken (sequel to *Roll of Thunder, Hear My Cry*), by Mildred Taylor

4. Investigate the historical background of this novel. What was the plight of black Americans in Mississippi in the 1930's? How did they suffer from segregation and from extremist groups like the Ku Klux Klan?

5. Research the historical-fiction story based upon the life of an important Afro-American.

6. Discuss the effects of the Depression on the nation as a whole and on blacks living in the rural South in particular.

7. Evaluate the use of *Roll of Thunder, Hear My Cry* as the title for this novel.

8. Along with members of your cooperative learning group, role-play a favorite scene in the story. Perform the scene for your classmates.

9. Set up a mock trial for the Wallaces and the Simmses. Appoint defense and prosecuting attorneys. Call Mr. Jamison, Mr. Avery, the Logan children and others to the stand as witnesses to testify about their brutal treatment of T.J.

10. Create a sequel to *Roll of Thunder, Hear My Cry*. What happens to the members of the Logan family? Do they retain the family land? Do their educational opportunities improve? Do they begin to have better relationships with their neighbors? What happens to T.J.? Give your tale an imaginative title. Illustrate your tale.

Glossary of Literary Terms

Alliteration: A repetition of initial, or beginning, sounds in two or more consecutive or neighboring words.

Analogy: A comparison based upon the resemblance in some particular ways between things that are otherwise unlike.

Anecdote: A short account of an interesting, amusing or biographical occurrence.

Anticlimax: An event that is less important than what occurred before it.

Archaic language: Language that was once common in a particular historic period but which is no longer commonly used.

Cause and effect: The relationship in which one condition brings about another condition as a direct result. The result, or consequence, is called the effect.

Character development: The ways in which the author shows how a character changes as the story proceeds.

Characterization: The method used by the author to give readers information about a character; a description or representation of a person's qualities or peculiarities.

Classify: To arrange according to a category or trait.

Climax: The moment when the action in a story reaches its greatest conflict.

Compare and contrast: To examine the likenesses and differences of two people, ideas or things. (*Contrast* always emphasizes differences. *Compare* may focus on likenesses alone or on likenesses and differences.)

Conflict: The main source of drama and tension in a literary work; the discord between persons or forces that brings about dramatic action.

Connotation: Something suggested or implied, not actually stated.

Description: An account that gives the reader a mental image or picture of something.

Dialect: A form of language used in a certain geographic region; it is distinguished from the standard form of the language by pronunciation, grammar and/or vocabulary.

Dialogue (dialog): The parts of a literary work that represent conversation.

Fact: A piece of information that can be proven or verified.

Figurative language: Description of one thing in terms usually used for something else. Simile and metaphor are examples of figurative language.

Flashback: The insertion of an earlier event into the normal chronological sequence of a narrative.

Foreshadowing: The use of clues to give readers a hint of events that will occur later on.

Historical fiction: Fiction represented in a setting true to the history of the time in which the story takes place.

Imagery: Language that appeals to the senses; the use of figures of speech or vivid descriptions to produce mental images.

© **Educational Impressions, Inc.**

Irony: The use of words to express the opposite of their literal meaning.

Legend: A story handed down from earlier times; its truth is popularly accepted but cannot be verified.

Limerick: A humorous five-lined poem with a specific form: aabba. Lines 1, 2 and 5 are longer than lines 3 and 4.

Metaphor: A figure of speech that compares two unlike things without the use of like or as.

Mood: The feeling that the author creates for the reader.

Motivation: The reasons for the behavior of a character.

Narrative: The type of writing that tells a story.

Narrator: The character who tells the story.

Opinion: A personal point of view or belief.

Parody: Writing that ridicules or imitates something more serious.

Personification: A figure of speech in which an inanimate object or an abstract idea is given human characteristics.

Play: A literary work that is written in dialogue form and that is usually performed before an audience.

Plot: The arrangement or sequence of events in a story.

Point of view: The perspective from which a story is told.

Protagonist: The main character.

Pun: A play on words that are similar in sound but different in meaning.

Realistic fiction: True-to-life fiction; the people, places and happenings are similar to those in real life.

Resolution: The part of the plot from the climax to the ending where the main dramatic conflict is worked out.

Satire: A literary work that pokes fun at individual or societal weaknesses.

Sequencing: The placement of story elements in the order of their occurrence.

Setting: The time and place in which the story occurs.

Simile: A figure of speech that uses *like* or *as* to compare two unlike things.

Stereotype: A character whose personality traits represent a group rather than an individual.

Suspense: Quality that causes readers to wonder what will happen next.

Symbolism: The use of a thing, character, object or idea to represent something else.

Synonyms: Words that are very similar in meaning.

Tall tale: An exaggerated story detailing unbelievable events.

Theme: The main idea of a literary work; the message the author wants to communicate, sometimes expressed as a generalization about life.

Tone: The quality or feeling conveyed by the work; the author's style or manner of expression.

ANSWERS

Chapters One and Two: Vocabulary

1. F.	5. A	9. R	13. D	17. S
2. M	6. T	10. C	14. H	18. L
3. K	7. B	11. I	15. E	19. G
4. P	8. N	12. O	16. J	20. Q

Chapter One: Comprehension and Discussion Questions (Answers may vary.)

1. Papa had to work on the railroad so that they would have enough money to pay the taxes on the 400 acres and the mortgage that remained on 200 of the acres. The cotton was not enough. Although he would have preferred to remain with his family, it was important to all of them that they keep the land.

2. The Great Faith Elementary and Secondary School didn't begin until October so that the children—and the teachers—could work the cotton fields during the summer harvest. Likewise, the school term ended in March so that they could work the fields during the spring months.

3. The schools were segregated. Great Faith had no school buses; Jefferson Davis did. Great Faith had a wide crabgrass lawn; Jefferson Davis had an expansive front lawn with a Mississippi flag and an American flag (transposed so that the American flag was on the bottom!). Great Faith consisted of 4 weather-beaten wooden houses; Jefferson Davis was a long, white wooden building. Jefferson Davis had a wide sports field with tiered benches; Great Faith had none. The students in Jefferson Davis all had books. The children at Great Faith were surprised that they were to have any books, although they were disappointed when they saw their condition. The children at Jefferson Davis had books in good condition. Great Faith only had a small potbellied stove; the heating system at Jefferson Davis isn't described. Only a curtain divided the classrooms at Great Faith.

4. Mama understood why the children had reacted as they did. She glued paper over the offensive labels. When Miss Crocker said that sometimes the children have to learn how things are, Mama replied, "That doesn't mean they have to accept them...and maybe we don't either."

Chapter Two: Comprehension and Discussion Questions (Answers may vary.)

1. Papa explained that Mr. Morrison hadn't been able to find work since he was fired from the railroad. Although that might have been true, it was probably also true—as Stacey suspected—that he wanted Mr. Morrison to be there to protect the family while he was away, especially after he had heard about the burnings.

2. "Sorry, Cassie girl, but I stay any longer, I might lose my job," he explained.

3. After being accused of flirting with a white woman, he had been chased down and set afire.

4. The older children went there to dance and smoke and drink. Papa knew that the Wallaces didn't like or respect the black children and he was afraid they would get into trouble. Although the statement seemed disconnected with the conversation, the talk about the burnings probably made Papa worry about possible trouble with whites.

Chapters Three and Four: Vocabulary

1. distant [in interest]; indifferent (Chap. 4, Par. 66)
2. train of vehicles (Chap. 3, Par. 208)
3. lurched; swerved (Chap. 3, Par. 88)
4. babying; pampering (Chap. 3, Par. 10)
5. put on clothing (Chap. 3, Par.3)
6. pretended (Chap. 4, Par. 39)
7. worn and tired (Chap. 3, Par. 166)
8. with arrogance and vanity (Chap. 4, Par. 31)
9. stupid; foolish (Chap. 3, Par. 37)
10. tormenting (Chap. 3, Par. 17)
11. fixed; held attention (Chap. 4, Par. 36)
12. changed direction (Chap.3, Par. 36)
13. expressed at risk of criticism (Chap. 3, Par. 93)
14. irritate; annoy (Chap. 4, Par. 180)
15. floated gently through the air (Chap. 3, Par. 37)

Chapter Three: Comprehension and Discussion Questions (Answers may vary.)

1. Little Man liked to keep himself neat and clean. Also, the others were more used to the humiliation; they had been through it before. Little Man was not used to it.

2. Although Jeremy was white, he didn't really get along with the other white children and he preferred to be with the Logan children. Perhaps he understood that the behavior of the other white children was wrong and cruel. Perhaps he himself felt like an outcast among them for reasons we are not told.

3. The children dug a large trench in the muddy road. When the rain filled the trench, the hole turned into a trap. The bus careened into the ditch and was broken—pretty much according to plan. The children had forgotten, however, that others—namely Mama—could have fallen into the ditch if they had gotten there before the bus.

4. Mr. Avery had come to warn Mama about the night riders. The children thought that the night riders had found out about their involvement in the bus incident and were coming to get them.

© Educational Impressions, Inc.

Chapter Four: Comprehension and Discussion Questions (Answers may vary.)

1. The children now knew that the night riders hadn't been looking for them.

2. Stacey had taken away the set of cheating notes that T.J. had prepared. When Mrs. Logan found the notes, she assumed that they were Stacey's because Stacey wouldn't tell on T.J.

3. Mr. Morrison felt that the children should admit what they had done and that they should take responsibility for their actions. Stacey announced that he would tell Mama himself and from then on Stacey and Mr. Morrison seemed to have a greater respect for one another.

4. Mrs. Logan wanted her children to understand the danger of consorting with people like the Wallaces. She knew that seeing Mr. Berry burnt and scarred would have a greater impact upon them than any punishment they might receive.

Chapters Five and Six: Vocabulary

1. walked slowly (Chap. 5, Par. 78)
2. resisted; refused abruptly (Chap.5, Par. 99)
3. lacking distinctive characteristics (Chap. 5, Par. 51)
4. wavered in confidence (Chap. 5, Par. 97)
5. weakly; with little animation (Chap. 6, Par. 157)
6. with ill will (Chap. 5, Par. 73)
7. neatly; smartly (Chap. 6, Par. 9)
8. offensive (Chap. 5, Par. 6)
9. with awe and respect (Chap. 6, Par. 139)
10. criticism or censure for a fault (Chap. 6, Par. 68)
11. unwillingly (Chap. 5, Par. 45)
12. returned evil for evil (Chap. 5, Par. 72)
13. quiet (Chap. 5, Par. 7)
14. sulkily; with resentment (Chap. 5, Par. 77)
15. was moodily silent & irritable (Chap. 6, Par.1)

Chapter Five: Comprehension and Discussion Questions (Answers may vary.)

1. Mr. Jamison treated them with respect. Unlike other whites, Mr. Jamison addressed Mama and Big Ma as "Missus." Also, she noted that when asked a question, he gave a straight answer—just like her father.

2. Mr. Barnett finally waited on Cassie and Stacey after keeping them waiting for a long time; however, when a white girl—no older than Cassie—came over, he stopped waiting on them to take care of the white girl. When Cassie expressed her annoyance, Mr. Bartlett called her a "little nigger."

3. He knew that T.J. wouldn't have the nerve to say anything to antagonize the white folks. "Don't worry 'bout T.J. He knows exactly how to act."

4. Big Ma was probably afraid that Mr. Simms would harm Cassie if she didn't apologize. He had already threatened not to let them go unless Cassie apologized.

Chapter Six: Comprehension and Discussion Questions (Answers may vary.)

1. Answers will vary.

2. Hammer knew that Cassie had been hurt emotionally, if not physically, by Mr. Simms. Also, he resented the fact that he and other blacks had fought in the war but that they were denied basic respect.

3. "He's one of those people who has to believe that white people are better...to make himself feel big." She also explained that when slavery became very profitable, many people "decided to believe that black people really weren't people like everybody else." She went on to say that people like Mr. Simms hold onto that belief harder...because they have little else to hold on to."

4. The Wallaces had mistaken Uncle Hammer for Mr. Granger. Mama believed that the Wallaces would get even with them for embarrassing them.

Chapters Seven and Eight: Vocabulary

1. bewildered	4. wry	7. sentinels	10. astonishment	13. denotes
2. encounter	5. distastefully	8. inaudible	11. briskly	14. interjected
3. obvious	6. adorned	9. flaunting	12. resentful	15. acknowledged

Chapter Seven: Comprehension and Discussion Questions (Answers may vary.)

1. Both were upset and somewhat hurt that he had given away the jacket. Mama wanted Stacey to go and get the coat back. Not only did she know that she and Papa couldn't afford to get him another, but she also felt badly that he had given away a gift from a loved one. She was surprised that Hammer told him to leave the jacket where it was. Hammer probably wanted to teach him to accept the consequences of his actions and to think for himself. "What the devil should he care what T.J. thinks or T.J. says?" "As long as there are people, there's gonna be somebody trying to take what you got and trying to drag you down."

2. The mood created by the author was warm and inviting. Papa was home for the holiday. There were many special foods being prepared: sweet-potato pies, custard pies, pound cakes, raccoon with yams and onions, and a ham. The house was decorated with pines and holly with bright red berries. Peanuts were roasting in the fire. The

feelings of happiness and contentment, however, became mixed with feelings of sadness as the family sat around and told stories about the past.

3. Papa wanted them to know their history, even though much of what they were about to hear would cause them pain and sorrow and would probably frighten them.

4. Mr. Jamison had agreed to back the credit for 30 families to shop in Vicksburg instead of at the Wallaces' store, in which Mr. Granger had a financial interest. Mr. Granger warned them that if they continued to cause trouble, he would see to it that they lose their land. "Mr. Joe Higgins up at First National told me that he couldn't hardly honor a loan to folks who go around stirring up a lot of bad feelings in the community—"

Chapter Eight: Comprehension and Discussion Questions (Answers may vary.)

1. Papa explained that sometimes we must do things we don't like and that we have to make decisions about what is and is not worth fighting for. He told her that there are some things that eat away at you if you don't do anything about them and that she had to decide whether or not her relationship with Lillian Jean was one of those things. He also warned her that if Mr. Simms got involved, it would bring him (Papa) into it and there would be real trouble.

2. Cassie doted on Lillian Jean and pretended to be her "slave." Lillian often confided in her about her friends. Then, when least expected, Cassie led Lillian Jean into the woods and threw down her books. When Lillian slapped Cassie, Cassie retaliated by knocking her down and beating her. She forced Lillian to apologize by threatening to reveal to Lillian's friends all the secrets she had been told.
Cassie had obviously decided that she wouldn't have been able to live with herself if she hadn't resolved her relationship with Lillian Jean.

3. He had Mama fired for teaching about slavery and for damaging the books.

4. T.J. had told Kaleb Wallace that Mama had destroyed the books and that she was stopping people from shopping in his store. Stacey made sure that everyone knew it was T.J. who had gotten Mrs. Logan fired. None of their friends would talk to T.J.

Chapters Nine and Ten: Vocabulary

1. in an unyielding manner (Chap. 10, Par. 176)
2. social courtesies (Chap. 9, Par. 66)
3. with a superior air (Chap. 10, Par. 201)
4. with a sense of hopelessness (Chap. 9, Par. 174)
5. with a sense of hopelessness (Chap. 10, Par. 53)
6. irritation; annoyance (Chap. 9, Par. 118)
7. wrinkled (Chap. 9, Par. 124)
8. without precise limits (Chap. 9, Par. 2)
9. book of monetary transactions (Chap. 10, Par. 2)
10. sluggishly (Chap. 10, Par. 80)
11. contract (Chap. 10, Par. 135)
12. cast a shadow over (Chap. 9, Par. 93)
13. enduring (Chap. 10, Par. 96)
14. occurring before usual (Chap. 9, Par. 121)
15. accepted as inevitable (Chap. 9, Par. 56)
16. systematic, orderly design (Chap. 10, Par. 134)
17. in an ill-at-ease manner (Chap. 9, Par. 80)
18. send for (Chap. 9, Par. 45)
19. harmonizing exactly (Chap. 10, Par. 149)
20. pressing importance (Chap. 10, Par. 59)

Chapter Nine: Comprehension and Discussion Questions (Answers may vary.)

1. Mr. Jamison wanted to warn the Logans that Thurston Wallace was in town "talking 'bout how he's not gonna let a few smart colored folks ruin his business." Most of the children will probably consider Mr. Jamison a friend.

2. Mr. Granger told the men they would have to give him 60 percent of their cotton instead of 50 percent. He also threatened to force them off his land and to have the sheriff put them on the chain gang to work off their debts. The men feared for the well-being of their families.

3. Answers will vary, but Papa probably wanted Stacey to be prepared to head the family should harm come to Papa. "I want him to know...how to take care of things when I ain't around."

4. Stacey thought it was his fault because when the men shot at Papa, Jack reared up and Stacey wasn't strong enough to hold the reins tightly. The wagon rolled over Papa's leg. Most will probably feel that Stacey was not to blame.

Chapter Ten: Comprehension and Discussion Questions (Answers may vary.)

1. They feared that Hammer's temper would get out of hand if he learned what happened to Papa. "Things like they are, he come down here wild and angry, he'll get himself hung." Papa changed his mind when Harlan Granger convinced the bank to make his loan due and payable immediately even though Papa had four years left on his mortgage.

2. Mr. Morrison had checked to make sure Mr. Wallace didn't have a gun with him. He knew that without a gun Mr. Wallace was too much of a coward to act alone.

© **Educational Impressions, Inc.**

3. Answers will vary, but most readers were probably not surprised.

4. T.J. brought the white boys to show off to his old friends. He wanted them to see that he was hanging out with rich white boys who bought him presents. He didn't realize that the boys were just using him.

Chapters Eleven and Twelve: Vocabulary

Part 1
1. oration
2. plod
3. prolonged
4. surged
5. leftovers
6. violently
7. threateningly
8. defenselessness

Part 2
1. decrease
2. enter
3. denial
4. mildly
5. likable
6. lightheartedly
7. aware
8. trustingly

Chapter Eleven: Comprehension and Discussion Questions (Answers may vary.)

1. "Stacey had felt a responsibility for T.J....Perhaps he felt that even a person as despicable as T.J. needed someone he could call 'friend,' or perhaps he sensed T.J.'s vulnerability better than T.J. did himself." Cassie went to "make sure he [Stacey] got back in one piece." The other two went because they didn't want to be left behind.

2. Answers will vary, but the children probably thought that T.J. was right when he said, "You go wakin' your grandmama and your daddy'll be in it." They didn't want their family to get involved and possibly be injured.

3. Mr. Jamison argued that the sheriff should be responsible for justice. The sheriff told the crowd that Mr. Granger did not want a hanging on his land.

4. The mob had threatened to go to their house and get Papa and Mr. Morrison. Also, the children thought that Papa would know what to do.

Chapter Twelve: Comprehension and Discussion Questions (Answers may vary.)

1. At first their parents thought the children had disobeyed by staying out late. When they learned what had happened, they realized the urgency of the situation.

2. Mr. Jamison suspected that Papa had something to do with starting the fire and he didn't want people to start thinking about it and come to the same conclusion. Answers will vary as to the wisdom of starting the fire.

3. Although we are never really told what T.J.'s punishment was, we can probably assume the worst. When Stacey asked if T.J. could die, Papa answered that he wished he could lie and tell them that he wouldn't.

4. Answers will vary.

Crossword Puzzle: